RAGGEDY PRAYERS AND CROOKED LADDERS

ALSO FROM UUMSB:

Poems of Prayer and Heresy
by Jan Hutchinson
drawings by Chet Kalm

A Memory of New Hunger:
A Gathering Of Writings
from members of
the congregation.

UUMSB
P.O. Box 423
Great Barrington, MA 01230
www.uumsb.org

Raggedy Prayers
and
Crooked Ladders

Jan Hutchinson

Drawings by Chet Kalm

UNITARIAN UNIVERSALIST MEETING OF SOUTH BERKSHIRE

Great Barrington, Massachusetts

UUMSB
P.O. Box 423
Great Barrington, MA 01230
www.uumsb.org
uumsb@yahoo.com

To order additional copies of this title, contact UUMSB at
the above email address.

Book and cover design by José García.

First Edition: 2013
ISBN: 978-1-4936-4289-2

To Vera Kalm

ACKNOWLEDGEMENTS

The poems in this collection were not written for an audience but as part of an on-going early morning poetry practice in which an almost childlike voice addresses the ineffable mysteries. These poems love the world, laugh at themselves, and honor the fluidity of truth.

José, Chet, and I dedicate this volume to Vera Kalm, who, with her steady and gracious insistence, was the driving force behind the project. We had to sneak the dedication in because Vera, in her humility, would never have agreed to it.

Chet outdid himself with his beautiful, whimsical drawings. It is an honor to work with Chet, an honor even to know Chet. His drawings and the poems seem to dance together.

José García enhanced the dance with his imaginative, careful layout and design. José worked with great patience, love, and skill in his typography, scanning, placement, and cover design to perfect the look of the book.

Thanks to those friends and family members who read this collection ahead and gave me helpful comments on the poems: Chet and Vera, of course, and also Jan Lawry, Meg Hutchinson, Belle Fox-Martin, and Lisa Maras.

Special thanks to the wise Sarah Hutchinson Hardcastle who, beyond her astute suggestions on the poems themselves, made particularly helpful notes on the arc of the poems in this collection.

All profits from the sale of this book will benefit the Unitarian Universalist Meeting of South Berkshire, a community in which "a free and responsible search for truth and meaning" is always respected, and truth's fluidity is expected.

Jan
December 2013

CONTENTS

SECTION I
IN THE BEGINNING WAS THE POEM

SECTION II
RAGGEDY PRAYERS

SECTION III
YES TO EVERYTHING

SECTION IV
LOSS, LIMPING, AND CHANGE

SECTION V
EVEN THE SILENCE IS A POEM

SECTION I

IN THE BEGINNING WAS THE POEM

3/18/2009

Everything means what it seems,
but there are secret trapdoors.

The words settle onto the page
and fold their wings a moment.

Strangers sit next to one another
on a train moving below hidden stars.

It is a time of angels.
All the paper money has left on the wind.

You can pray now
or wait forever
for proof
of God.

2/1/2009

Let's get out of the way
and see if the poem
will carry his own suitcase.

Oh look, he's dragging it along,
all overstuffed, but he's feeling private.
He uses his case as a footrest on the train.

If he's just going to hoard images,
let's take this moment to pray.
Petitions are a misuse of prayer.

Otherwise we could ask for help
in learning an elegant frugality
and a gratitude which burgeons.

What we wanted from the suitcase
was a picture or two,
something as simple as
a red handkerchief waved
from the now disappearing
caboose.

8/31/2010

What is it to be
a self in the world,
and how does poetry help?

Here in this now,
with the past gone
and the future unknowable,

we are in our little rowboats
on a great, chaotic
ocean of emotion,
lifting and dropping.

It is imagination
that lets us hold the oars
and believe our rowing matters.

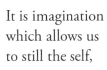

It is imagination
which allows us
to still the self,

to still the sea
and call it God.

4/9/2007

Start in the middle of nowhere,
which is probably where you are.

Take off your assumptions
and throw them to the winds.

Allow your senses to be raw
and open as a child's.

Let wonder wash you,
laugh at your awkward,

funny self, and sing
a new song of joy and thanks.

You are still alone
in the middle of nowhere,

but now you're laughing,
now you're singing,

now you're looking around
for God.

6/3/2009

Let's make a long pier
out of short words.
When we arrive
at the far end,
only ocean beyond,
we'll step off
either to sink
or flip over
onto our backs,
eyes to the sky.

Let's float beyond
the intellect,
that posturer,
and ego, so self-conscious.

Let's trust
our buoyant
hearts.

11/22/2009

Of course the sky
is simply itself
and its blue
only an illusion
of light passing through
our atmosphere.

Of course God,
if God exists,
is beyond perception
except through
the lifted heart's
wild windows.

Since religion
is only metaphor
anyway, it's okay
to throw our hearts
toward the infinite eye
of the flying sky.

3/18/2007

Let's get back
to the rules which state
the poems must be short,
the self left out
to circle the periphery.

Leave the center open
to allow the wild
rush of sky.

If the heart rises up
to sail on the wind,
how lovely.

If it lodges in a tree,
follow your kite string,
winding as you go.

Climb and retrieve
your flying heart.
Mend its tail of rags.

Prepare it for flight
again tomorrow.

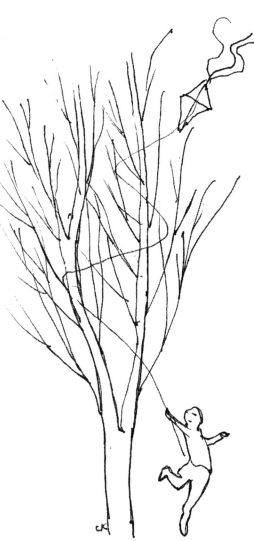

1/18/2009

Sometimes we wait
beside the white page,
not certain how to begin.

The target area is huge —
anything goes — aim for the If-God
or a tiny sparkling particular.

The essential element
is the heart engaged —
how it climbs atop the words

To fly out over clean snowfields.
Watch it wing into white distance.
Hear its laughter recede.

3/20/2012

Untangle your heart.
Now throw
the newly freed line
out across the chasm.

Step off onto your line.
Trust yourself and the wire
you have drawn on air.

It is this simple to become
an aerial artist,
a wire walker,

balancing upon
imagination alone.

4/23/2012

The Thread Exercise

An academic poet called me foolish
for believing writing poetry
can make us better people.

Yet the Buddhist Lama said just that:
Creativity of the right sort
leads to transformation.

Let's follow the thread of poetry,
hand over hand through
attention to loving particulars,

out into wide new spaces
of empty innerness
filled with light.

SECTION II

RAGGEDY PRAYERS

When your airplane
lifts off the runway,
you clutch the armrest
and think how bizarre it is,
how it defies imagination —
you ride in an enormous
metal flying machine
careening high above earth.

But what about these billions
of humans, walking upright
on a whirling ball in space,
surrounded by a fathomless
dark vacuum?
Now clutch your armrest!

If God does not exist,
let's make one up,
so we're not alone,
so that love surrounds us
on our spinning way.

3/1/2009

I still intend to pray
in my muddled way
even if God's not out there
in the sky and wind.

So what if the One who wove
the web of all being
is not a personal God
or even a good listener;

the force of the spirit
still takes my breath away.
An inexplicable magnet
still pulls at my heart.

God-Beyond-Religion
Who called us up through evolution,
casting off false forms,
shaping through eons
a vessel for spirit
in which to pour
a molten river of light,

If You exist that is,
it seems we are
a failed experiment,
holding instead greed and desire.
We plunder the earth jewel
and move against one another
with ever fiercer, more fiery weapons.

If-God, make me a servant
of Your glorious intention,
even if I have imagined it
and You.

9/24/2008

Great Holy,
imagined or not,
with or without You
it's an awesome miracle.

This ball of rock
with a molten heart
twirls in limitless
vacuum night
around a fire object.

There's a magnet of sorts,
gravity,
which holds us
on for the ride,

while that other magnet,
in our hearts,
pulls us toward You,
Great Holy,
imagined or not.

3/21/2009

Holy Longing,
lift me out
of my wooden chair
into the singing mysteries
beyond the sight of eyes.

I don't expect answers
and feel foolish
when my eager heart
shinnies up to my mind
where it dilutes itself
forever voicing questions.

If-God, make my heart content
where no answers are.
Let the longing
and its gift
of expansiveness
be the fullness of emptiness,
the presence of absence,
the all-encompassing,
totally mysterious,
Enough
in the opening now.

6/5/2005

Some people claim
to know The Truth.

Do I know the sun
because it shines on my arm
in my tree fort
on the raggedy edge
of a minor village
in the hilly, less inhabited end
of a small state
in an enormous country
on a vast planet of billions of souls
so many miles from our home star?

All the truths we're warmed by
are only shards and beams,
only splinters and glimpses.

The Truth
is the mind of God.

12/23/2011

At the heart of me
is the heart of You
opening into Yes.

It is love
that holds us on
this whirling planet.

Pooh-pooh I say
to matters of fact
like gravity.

Often the truths of science
don't mesh with
the truths of soul.

No worries, no conflict.
It's all true and not true
simultaneously.

At the heart of You
is the heart of me
opening into yes.

11/23/2009

Holy-Highness,
distant and near,
deliver me from answers.
Let me swim,
heart buoyant,
across the ocean
of the sky,
my questions pinwheeling
into exhausted silence.

Then let me
lie back and float
on longing's
very fullness
with itself…

And perhaps with You,
Endless Mystery,
Pure Essence.

Sweet sacred thread,
which unites the struggling particulars
into the Great Oneness,
allow the humble dream
of flying with you
in and out
through all the openings,
singing praise and delight.

May our over-eager minds
follow our earnest hearts.
May we crack our shells of self
to hatch out into the Whole.

May we sew compassion
with heart-rich simplicity
through this complex,
divided world.

9/13/2007

Here comes
another beautiful day
in which to learn
to get beyond myself
and buoy those about me,

To try to hold my heart
high and clear so
Your reflected light,
Mysterious Joy,
shines off me
into the world.

I want to serve the good.
I want to live the love.
I want to sing the joy
that is Yours,
High Holy Whatever,
Verb-God
bouncing.

2/13/2009

Let's open the window
in the page of prayer
and look far out
through the windy world
to where the sky flies
and the white pines dance.

You, Infinite
Magnet of Mystery,
keep us standing at our windows,
leaning our hearts out wide
through the hum and moan
of wind and wildness

while our small songs
break apart
and fly to meet the sky.

4/8/2010

Great Holy,
I am
high on wonder
and befuddled
by the improbability
of our existence.

Not Yours,
but mine this time,
my race and the myriad creatures,
the burgeoning green of April.

Help me never to disappear
into the pedestrian trudging
through days,
but always to stand
at the windows
of my heart,
clapping hands,
shouting WOW!
and laughing out loud.

12/21/2009

Great Holy,
I am naked here
in Your world,
stripped of any pride
amid my crumbling memories,
my unreliable perceptions.

Show me the footpath forward
from this difficult moment
into loving, useful work
for my final days
or decades.

Help me to release
what I thought was true
so that bright new truths
settle all around me
and eat from my hand
before they too
lift up and wing away.

SECTION III

YES TO EVERYTHING

10/21/2010

Time gallops forward
with long streamers
rippling back
into what came before.

As we grow old,
the streamers tatter
and tangle, so it's hard
to distinguish

The world's reality
from what the soul alone knows.
If we're lucky,
there's an alchemy,

A braiding of realities,
the inner and the outer,
into a golden cord
linking us to sacred Yes.

9/24/2010

Unimaginable Yes,
filling the sky
and racing all around us
in rivulets pulled
toward Your ocean,

It's all mysterious,
beyond understanding,
this desire which isn't desire,
this longing which is
its own fulfillment.

We don't need answers
or certainty,
we just step to the edge
of our egos
and dive out,

Entering cleanly
the calm silence
of the inexpressible.

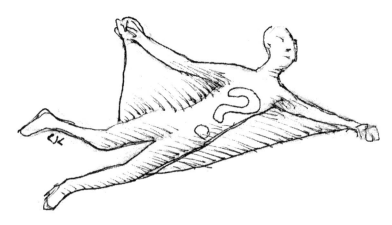

10/26/2010

Yes-God
pours everywhere
in and through this world
that science tries to explain.

A child's God would laugh,
throw back His head,
flip His white beard
in amongst roiling clouds.

As adults we live
with greater subtlety,
more mellow wonder,
less certainty.

But if we're lucky,
our emptiness opens —
we move on through
and emerge into

a new, wise, elder innocence.

11/12/2010

Often we forge off
into the future
without a ticket.
Maybe we'll gain admittance,
maybe we won't.

Learn to love
the little confusions
the way you honor
the Great Mysteries.

All security
is only illusion —
you know that.

Always there is
just as much Yes
as we muster the presence
to perceive.

4/4/2011

Although the snake
beguiled me
and I ate,

I am not
abandoned,
not banished.

In each moment
from every corner
of the garden,

The crooked ladders
still stretch up
into high-flying Yes.

12/1/2011

Whoever
you are,
however
you've fallen
short,

First,
with gratitude
and humility,
say yes
to your self,
to your life,

Then see
how the Great Yes
all around you
opens.

Imagine,
when need be,
the rickety,
crooked ladder
rising
from the blue-walled
garden of the moods.

Climb up it now,
hand over hand,
heart lifting
toward
the wild skies
of Yes.

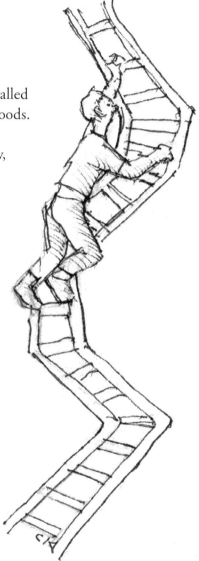

SECTION IV

LOSS, LIMPING, AND CHANGE

1/27/2005

Small losses come to remind us
of all that can be lost.

So silly to mourn a possession misplaced
when we own far too much.

And when, out in the darkness
beyond the campfires of comfort,

The great shaggy griefs circle
and growl low in their throats.

The thing to do today is add a log,
scoot closer to those you love
around your small fire in the wild dark.

When, one at a time, the losses press in,
treat them like expected guests.
Scratch behind their ears, and let
the songs continue.

12/13/2009

At last we bump up
against the ragged truth
that for all the specialness
we once felt inside,
the lives we've lived
are small and ordinary.

We neglected to blow enough
on the incipient flames.
We've had a job
instead of a career.
We've let fear clip our generosity.

There is still a chance
to make good
on the final challenge —
to arise through late life losses
with a loving Grace.

12/18/2009

Let's love and forgive
those awkward parts
of ourselves
which limp or stutter
or can't see clearly.

Let's inch forward,
always toward
our perception
or imagination
of goodness and light.

Aren't we all just
handicapped saints
on a world-wide
walking pilgrimage
of the wounded
and well-meaning?

2/18/2004

In the end we lose everything,
but that is not the point,
unless, of course, you choose
to chew your heart
and fall through bitten holes
into endless whistling dark.

Let's sit by the fire,
cross-legged here on earth.
Know any jokes?
Then let's sing off key.

We're laughing around
a flickering speck
on a dark mote
whirling in black space.

Oh yes there's gravity,
but love and levity
really hold us here.

1/9/2012

This day in the parade
of days waves its own
high flag of uniqueness.

The long parade winds out
of darkness on toward darkness,
mystery before and after.

It's getting quieter up front
after raucous youth, and
industrious middle age —

The gray-haired,
quiet years present the time
and mood for amazement.

We can see right through each
other to where wisdom sings
around campfires of soul.

2/11/2007

Just when the body gets old
and loses its spring,
the soul stands up
and asks it to dance.

"What Can't Be Known"
is another synonym for God,
Who plays the fiddle
just out of sight.

Spin till the ground
is smooth around you.
Follow the soul's lead.
Let the old feet frolic
toward Divine Presence,
which is what the soul
wanted
all along.

3/31/2007

Some man on the car radio announced
that the universe doesn't owe us
meaning. A news flash,

that's how I treated it,
but, of course, he's right.
We've already been given

more than enough of sunrise,
roses, ever-varied snowflakes,
birds of all color and song.

It's not up to the universe
to also lay out meaning.
That's why we're given

hearts and minds
to carry us beyond ourselves
deep into wonder and love.

Don't we, in effect,
owe the universe
meaning?

11/7/2009

If I were a child
with new fresh eyes
and ears clear of habit,
intellect, tradition,

I'd somersault out
between the bars of this cage
in bright pictures
onto the page,

Without any consciousness
of self,
without any stuckness,
without this limp and stammer,
without all the blather.
I'd swing my paintbrush
and dance my creations.

Don't worry
if I get raw
and run all wrinkly
out through
sparkling rain,
throwing off words.

Come with me.
Think of it as practice
for the grand finale.

1/17/2011

Listen for the sound
of children sledding
down the long hill
under the full moon.

They are squealing
with fear and excitement.
Like them we fly
over the bumps
and past the spilled ones.

Keep believing
in the journey.
Keep laughing
in the moonlight.

Everything lost
takes up its life
now within you.

1/31/2011

Whether or not
we know it,
we are all wabi-sabi,
like dented brass
or cracked crockery —
imperfect, irregular,
damaged, and elegant.

Joy and grief
walk hand in hand
out across the winter landscape.

So much must be lost
before we come
to a strong loneliness
in these white open fields.

11/26/2011

Water can't be broken —
trapped yes,
heated or cooled,
but water is strong
so it yields,
and left to its own
devices

Always flows
downhill,
singing as it goes,
toward the great
community,
the Ocean of Yes.

Even the clouds
are water.
Their sails filled with wind,
they are flying home.

Learn the lessons
of loss and change.
Be water.
Be unbroken.

12/2/2012

To stand outside
myself in judgment,
saying, "I am nothing"
is useless.

Let's first fill ourselves
with our selves
and the belief that
what we do matters.

Only then can we turn,
walk inward
toward the emptiness
where we truly become

Nothing.

10/22/2010

Back then on the long swim,
progress toward the island
seemed the purpose.

Slapping out the crawl,
we breathed deeply
and thrashed forward.

Maybe there is no island.
Maybe it's only the wonder,
the tenderness

With which we regard
the world, this life.
Perhaps the purpose

Was always buoyancy.

12/3/2012

Let's not let
the inevitable
vulnerability of aging
turn into fear.

Let's sit and observe
our vulnerability
from high up
in the lifeguard chair
of the witness self.

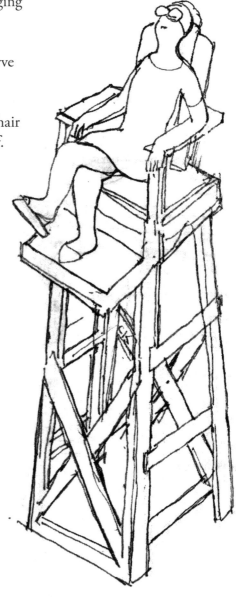

9/30/2009

We stand here
in our suits of flesh
holding out the sieve
of the years.

Either the mesh
is getting bigger
or whatever you might call
the falling stuff
is getting smaller,
falling faster.

We catch less these days.
It all sifts through.
But we're not sad, exactly,
in our wrinkle-suits
and silver hair,
just amazed
and increasingly quiet.

SECTION V

EVEN THE SILENCE IS A POEM

1/17/2009

Let's go in search
of the nearly silent poem
which delivers us
to the blue door

and smiles
gentle encouragement
as we struggle out
of our everyday thoughts

to try on
the ineffable
extraordinary,

always dancing
outside any circle
words can draw.

10/18/2011

Silence
is an open window
through which
the Great Mysteries
flow in and out
of our quiet hearts.

Whatever God is
speaks through
the emptiness
in the language
without sound.

May my heart become
an expansive ear,
listening ever more deeply
in through the heart
of silence.

5/27/2005

Open yourself
to the slow mystery
of silence.

Listen for the waters
lapping against the dock,
the creak and splash of oars,
the muffled voices
in the mist.

Sit still till the questions dissolve
and then the answers will arrive,
struggle up from their rowboat,
shake out cramped legs,
stretch to their full height,

Then they will hand you
a bundle of new questions,
wrapped in cloth and ribbon,
carried from across the water.

3/12/2010

Silence
is "the dream"
said the visiting musician.

Perhaps without it
music
becomes noise.

Poems
without pictures
are just ideas.

Ideas
without music
become blather.

The dream poem
is a picture
of silence.

12/31/2010

Let's banish the I
to the far wings,
unclutter the stage
into sweet openness.

And if no magnificent,
inexpressible reality
shows up to twirl
and hum and glow

in the poem's footlights,
at least there will be silence
and blessed emptiness,

waiting like a prayer.

11/22/2009

Let's let go
and tumble
into peace.

All these years
we've imagined
chaos

beneath
the tense struggle
to hold on.

Dreams
of falling
tried to tell us:

either
we will bounce
at the bottom

or wake up
in Time.

12/5/2011

I would
settle down
into the
simple
silence

where there is
no word
except
Open,

where everything —
my heart,
my mind,
the universe —

goes on
expanding
forever.

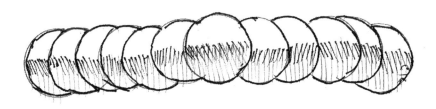

2/21/2009

Silence waits
beneath the great doing
and the undoing.

All the self-important
clapping of noise
sets up a din

to cloak the heartbeat,
the visceral rhythms,
in the inner cathedral.

My simple prayer
is only for awareness.
Be in me,

Silence.

10/24/2009

We know things beyond
what our brains know.

The heart waits below
the sieve of the mind

with a butterfly net
and gently captures

the pretty ideas
which filter through.

The heart is a hospital
for butterflies.

It is here where Grace
blows tenderly

until the delicate creatures
wake up and wing away.

Some scientists proclaim
reason to be the peak
of human evolution,

but what goes on
in the hospital of the heart
defies logic, trumps reason.

4/29/2010

Silence
is a huge,
majestic
lion.

I allow
the sacred paws
to walk
into my heart.

When the lion
leans down,
I climb up to straddle
his rippling back.

Now I hold
the golden mane
and ride
the silence.

4/6/2012

How sweet to define
success as simplification,
to head toward the quiet
instead of the applause.

We've been dancing
these many decades
and telling our stories on the edge
of the bed of language.

As if by inner direction now,
the words begin to inch
toward quiet simplicity.

We're so sophisticated,
you and I,
we're almost invisible.

2/18/2009

When we set out,
we have no idea
where we'll end up.

We spend decades
trying to find ourselves,
then the joke becomes clear:

We find ourselves only
to perceive at last
how the goal now flips

And is to lose the ego,
give the self to others,
expand the hearty innerness,

To wait in cathedral silence
while Everything Beyond
lights up in wonder.

Made in the USA
Columbia, SC
19 March 2018